Y0-DJN-765

GOLF

GOODYEAR
Physical Activities Series

Edited by J. Tillman Hall

Archery	Jean A. Barrett *California State University, Fullerton*
Badminton	James Poole *California State University, Northridge*
Bowling	Norman E. Showers *Southern Illinois University*
Fencing	Nancy L. Curry *Southwest Missouri State College*
Folk Dance	J. Tillman Hall *University of Southern California*
Golf	Edward F. Chui *University of Hawaii*
Handball	Pete Tyson *University of Texas*
Men's Basketball	Richard H. Perry *University of Southern California*
Men's Gymnastics	Gordon Maddux *California State University, Los Angeles*
Paddleball and Racquetball	A. William Fleming *Florida International University* Joel A. Bloom *University of Houston*
Soccer	John Callaghan *University of Southern California*
Social Dance	John G. Youmans *Temple University*

Swimming Donald L. Gambril
Harvard University

Fundamentals of Physical Education J. Tillman Hall
University of Southern California

Kenneth C. Lersten
University of Southern California

Merril J. Melnick
University of Southern California

Talmage W. Morash
California State University, Northridge

Richard H. Perry
University of Southern California

Robert A. Pestolesi
California State University, Long Beach

Burton Seidler
California State University, Los Angeles

Volleyball Randy Sandefur
California State University, Long Beach

Tennis Barry C. Pelton
University of Houston

Women's Basketball Ann Stutts
California State University, Northridge

Women's Gymnastics Mary L. Schreiber
California State University, Los Angeles

GOODYEAR PUBLISHING COMPANY, INC.
Pacific Palisades, California

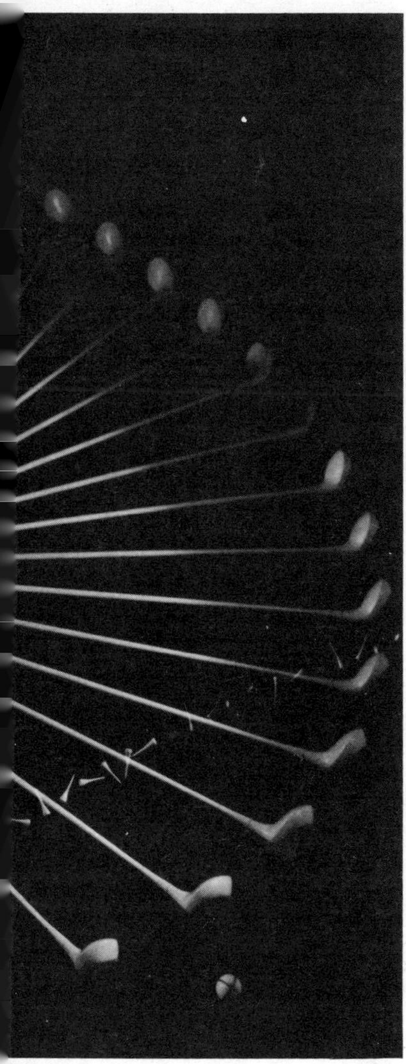

Goodyear Physical Activities Series
J. Tillman Hall: *Series Editor*

Edward F. Chui

University of Hawaii

SECOND EDITION

GOLF

Acknowledgments

I wish to acknowledge my appreciation to Dr. J. Tillman Hall for giving me the opportunity to publish this book, and to Dr. H. E. Edgerton of the Massachusetts Institute of Technology for graciously providing and allowing the use of his stroboscopic photographs. My thanks also to F. M. Yoshikami for his inspiring and professional advice.

Second Edition

Copyright © 1973, 1969 by
GOODYEAR PUBLISHING COMPANY, INC.
Pacific Palisades, California

All rights reserved. No part of this book may be reproduced in any form or by any means without permission in writing from the publisher.

Library of Congress Catalog Card Number: 72-91475

Current printing (last number):
10 9 8 7 6 5 4 3 2 1

ISBN: 0-87620-356-X
Y-356X-8
Printed in the United States of America
cover photo by Dr. H. E. Edgerton

Contents

Editor's note

The Goodyear Publishing Company presents a series of physical education books written by instructors expert in their respective fields.

These books on major sports are intended as supplementary material for the instructor and to aid the student in the understanding and mastery of the sport of his choice. Each book covers its fundamentals—the beginning techniques, rules and customs, equipment and terms—and gives to the reader the spirit of the sport.

Each author of this series brings to the reader the knowledge and skill he has acquired over many years of teaching and coaching. We sincerely hope that these books will prove invaluable to the college student or any student of the sport.

In GOLF, Edward Chui, Chairman of the Physical Education Department at the University of Hawaii, presents a complete analysis of the fundamentals of this great and popular sport.

The book begins with a brief and interesting history of the game, and continues with a thorough presentation of the terminology, equipment, etiquette, and rules, and presents to the student a clear and concise explanation of the execution of a variety of swings. To further aid the student in learning this sport suggestions for improvement, and review questions, are included. More than one hundred photographs and drawings will make this book more exciting than most on the subject, and will also help the student in learning correct grips, foot and body positions, and swings.

As a beginning player, or advanced player wanting to improve his game, GOLF will be fun to read while learning the correct way to play the game.

The tear-out student/teacher evaluation forms included in this revised book should be a real asset to both the teacher and the student.

Brief History and Background

ORIGIN OF THE GAME

In the fifteenth century, the Scots played a game that resembled modern golf. It became so widely popular among them that in 1457 James II and the Scottish Parliament decried and prohibited the game. They felt that golf jeopardized the nation's defense by diverting men from the more military sport of archery. Despite the royal ban, the game never was completely abandoned. The Scots' persistent interest in it led to its refinement to the point of using a small variety of clubs to knock a ball over a prescribed course toward a hole in the ground.

EARLY DEVELOPMENT

During the sport's early development in Scotland, the undulating seaside proved a well suited area for the game. The stretches of sand, covered with occasional plots of grass, were called links. The terrain offered not only sand dunes but also gullies, expanses of gentle hills, bluffs, and clusters of vegetation and shrubbery—all providing a series of natural hazards that added challenge to the game. In

1

the beginning, distance was not standardized; the players would simply start at some convenient spot and agree to play to some known hole. The number of holes usually varied from five to six. The game gradually grew more intensely competitive, and more holes were added. When the links were enlarged to include as many as twenty holes, the play became formalized to some degree. The clubs were made of single pieces of wood, crudely designed, with clubheads about six inches in length.

MODERN DEVELOPMENTS

The Clubs

The first important transition to modern golf was marked by the manufacture of the head of the club separately from the wooden shaft, these being joined by splicing. Gradually, the face of the wooden head was given loft, and names such as *brassie* and *spoon* emerged. Next came clubs with iron heads, which were designed and constructed to permit considerable variation in loft as well as greater adaptation to the wide diversity of playing conditions. Early in the 1920's, American golf club manufacturers introduced the tubular steel shaft. It was so readily accepted that the hickory wood shaft rapidly disappeared.

The Ball

The golf ball also has a history. Before 1848, the *feathery*, a ball made of feathers sewed into a leather case, was used. In 1848, the *gutty*, which was made from the gum of a *gutta-percha* tree, was introduced. The gutty was more solid, more resilient, more exciting to play, and considerably cheaper than the feathery ball. Then came refinements of the gutty. In about 1900, the Haskell rubber-cored ball, which was wrapped in *gutta-percha*, was successfully introduced. Before long, the solid rubber core was wrapped with strands of rubber and covered with a thinner layer of refined *gutta-percha*, with *balata* soon becoming available as a substitute for *gutta-percha*. At the same time, it was found that a ball with a smooth surface did not hold the line as well, and did not fly as far, as one that was nicked. As a result, surface grooves were cut in the balls. By 1930, round dimples replaced the grooves. Balls with solid rubber cores filled with liquid were produced experimentally. The steel-centered ball is a major variation upon the liquid-centered ball. Improvements in golf balls led to specifications for them in the official rules of the game.

FORERUNNERS OF MODERN GOLF COURSES

The great forerunner of modern golf courses was the Royal and Ancient Golf Club, at St. Andrews, Scotland, established in 1754. It still exists—as the oldest and most famous club in the history of golf. A century and a half later, the first golf club in the United States, the Oakhurst Golf Club, was founded by a group of men near White Sulphur Springs, in Greenbrier County, West Virginia. The Shinnecock Hills Golf Club, founded in 1891, was the first in the United States to erect a clubhouse and to secure a charter. The first 18-hole course in the United States was opened in 1893 by the Chicago Golf Club.

CHAMPIONSHIP TOURNAMENTS

The first British Open was held in 1860, with the first British Amateur following in 1885. The first USGA (United States Golf Association) Open was played in 1894. In the United States, the United States Golf Association, founded in 1894, is the official ruling body. The official authority in British golf is the Ancient and Royal Golf Club of St. Andrews.

Nature
of the
Game

2

Many ardent golfers, amateurs as well as professionals, have suggested that golf is essentially a simple game. This notion might be justified by saying that basically the game involves three physical tasks: driving the ball (to get distance), lofting the ball (for various flight trajectories), and rolling the ball. There are two objectives common to these three basic tasks—distance and direction. The challenge of the game, therefore, is to achieve accuracy in obtaining correct distance and true direction when driving, lofting, or rolling the ball. These objectives become one—to play the ball into a prescribed hole with the least number of strokes.

For the golfer who plays primarily for recreation, golf is simply a game. But not so for the golfer who has been bitten by the golf bug! This player takes the game seriously, to put it mildly. He literally eats and sleeps golf, is completely immersed in it. He talks golf continually. He insists that golf is really more than a game; it is a rigorous discipline. The evaluation of results rests upon a close relationship between a qualitative factor and a quantitative factor. The qualitative factor is excellence in execution of the stroke—the true swing and the finesse in making the necessary shots. It refers to the mechanical aspects of golf. The quantitative factor is the number of strokes a player executes, and the number of penalty strokes sustained in playing a hole. The serious golfer learns through experience that executing the true swing does not automatically turn out low scores. The perfection of physical ability must go hand in hand with a good mental and emotional outlook. The serious tournament player works for results that rest heavily upon effectiveness in scoring. He thinks of effectiveness in terms of 2s, 3s, 4s, and 5s. Any hole played with a score above a 5 would frustrate him. Thus, he practices, plays, studies, analyzes, and experiments to lower his score. He disciplines himself with the idea that golf is more than simply swinging a club correctly; it is a thinking person's game. Therefore, he works at perfection in execution and, at the same time, he learns to think through each situation and to apply sound strategy for low scores.

The standard golf course consists of a series of 18 holes, or units of play. The constituent parts of a hole of golf include the *teeing ground, through the green* (which contains the *fairway, roughs, obstructions,* and often trees), *hazards* (any *bunker* or *water hazard),* the *putting green,* and the *hole* with its *flagstick.* In some cases, there are *out-of-bounds* areas. The player starts each hole by playing his first stroke from the designated teeing ground, and then attempts to play the ball into the designated hole in the fewest number of strokes. Each hole is assigned a numerical value called par. There are par 3s, par 4s, and par 5s for men and for women. Occasionally, there are par 6s for women. The par for a hole usually is determined by the length of the hole measured from the teeing ground to the approximate center of the putting green. The player's general objective is to select and use the right club, stroke the ball with precision, and get it into the hole so as to equal or better the par for the hole. Par for a round of golf (18 holes of play) is a cumulative score of about 71 or 72, depending upon the particular golf course.

Figure 2.1 Views of several golf holes.

Terminology

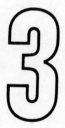

ACE   A score of "1" for a hole played.

ADDRESSING THE BALL   Taking one's stance in preparing to play the ball. Where the rules permit, this includes grounding the club.

ADVICE   Any counsel or suggestion that could influence a player in choosing a club or a method of playing a stroke.

APPROACH   The turfed passageway that leads from the fairway to the front opening of the green.

APPROACH SHOT   The stroke played to the putting green.

APRON   The closely cut grass area immediately surrounding the putting green. It is technically part of the fairway and not of the putting green.

AWAY   With two or more players, the player whose ball is farthest away from the hole is said to be away. That player has priority over others to play his next stroke first.

BACKSWING   The movement of the clubhead from the addressed position backward and upward preparatory to the forward swing.

BALL HOLED   A ball is holed when it lies within the circumference of the hole and entirely below the lip of the hole.

BALL IN PLAY   A ball is in play immediately following completion of the player's first stroke on the teeing ground.

BALL LOST   A ball is lost if the player is unable to find it within five minutes after he has begun to search for it, or when another ball has been put in play in accordance with the rules.

BIRDIE   The score for a hole played in one stroke less than par.

BITE   The action of the ball upon landing, usually on the putting green surface, giving the effect of gripping onto the surface and taking a firm hold at impact.

BOGEY   The score for a hole played in one stroke over par.

BRASSIE   The club designated as the No. 2 wood.

BUNKER   A type of hazard that serves as an obstacle, which often appears as a depression in the ground and is usually covered with sand.

CADDIE   A person who carries and handles a player's bag and clubs during the play of a round. The caddie is permitted to assist the player by rendering advice upon selecting clubs, reading the putting surface, and so on.

CARRY   The distance of a ball's flight between the position on the course where it is struck and the point where it first lands.

CASUAL WATER   A visible temporary accumulation of water that is not in a water hazard.

CHIP SHOT   A relatively short stroke played as an approach shot; the ball traveling with little flight and considerable roll.

COMPETITOR   A player in a stroke-play competition.

COURSE   The whole area within which play is permitted.

DIVOT   A piece of turf cut out by a club during a swing.

DOG-LEG   The portion of a fairway between teeing ground and the putting green where the direction in the course of play takes an angle from a straight line.

DORMIE   A scoring situation in which a side in match play is as many holes ahead of its opponent as the number of holes remaining to be played.

DOUBLE BOGEY   The score for a hole played in two strokes over par.

DOWN   The number of holes (in match play) or strokes (in stroke play) a player is behind his opponent or his fellow competitor.

DRAW   A flight pattern of the ball resembling a subtle form of the hook.

DRIVE   The stroke played for maximal distance; the driver ordinarily being used for the first stroke from the teeing ground.

DRIVER   The club designated as the No. 1 wood.

DROP   The act of putting the ball into play in accordance with the rules, in which the player faces the hole, stands erect, and drops the ball behind him over his shoulder.

DUB   A very poorly stroked shot resulting in the ball's traveling considerably less than the desired distance.

EAGLE   The score for a hole played in two strokes less than par.

ETIQUETTE   Conventional requirements of behavior and conduct by every player while on the course.

EXPLOSION SHOT   A vigorously executed stroke from an embedded lie, usually in sand.

FADE   A flight pattern resembling a subtle form of the slice.

FAIRWAY   The popular term for that portion of the hole through the green where the grass is short and the area free of obstacles.

FELLOW COMPETITOR   Any player in the stroke competition other than oneself.

FLIGHT   The aerial passage of the ball after it has been struck.

FLIGHT COMPETITION   The placement of players in groups arranged according to handicap ratings.

FORE   The warning called out to anyone who may be within range of play or near an approaching ball.

FOURBALL PLAY   Partners opposing other partners, each side playing its better ball; the ball with which the better score was made.

GREEN   The popular term for the putting green.

GRIP   (1) The part of the shaft of a club to which approved material may be added for the purpose of obtaining a firm hold; the handle of a club. (2) Manner of holding a club for the purpose of playing a stroke.

GROUND UNDER REPAIR   Any portion of the course so marked and including material piled for removal or a hole made by a greenkeeper.

HANDICAP   The number of artificial strokes a player receives to adjust his scoring ability to the common level of zero or scratch handicap golf. Handicaps are used to equate differentials in the abilities of opposing players.

HALVED   In match competition, a hole is halved when both sides have played the hole in the same number of strokes.

HAZARD   Any bunker, or water hazard such as any sea, lake, pond, river, or ditch.

HOLE   (1) A unit of play on the course; any one of eighteen. (2) A cavity (4¼" in diameter and at least 4" deep) made on the putting green to serve as the receiving target into which the player must play his ball.

HOLE OUT   The completion of play of a hole.

HONOR   The privilege to drive or play first from the teeing ground. This is given to the player with the lowest score on the preceding hole, or decided by lot.

HOOK   The flight pattern of a ball curving to the left of the straight line for a right-handed player, or curving to the right of the straight line for a left-handed player.

IRON   A club with a metal head.

LEVERAGE   The performance action of the arms and hands brought about by maintaining a straight left arm well into the follow-through and allowing the right hand to hinge pass the left hand during impact.

LIE   (1) The position, or situation, of the ball at rest. (2) The angle of the shaft of the club relative to the ground when the clubhead is grounded in its natural position.

LOFT   The slope, or inclination, of the face of the clubhead backward from the perpendicular.

LOOSE IMPEDIMENT   A natural object not fixed or growing and not adhering to the ball.

MARKER   (1) A person who is appointed to record a competitor's score.   (2) A ball marker — commonly a small coin placed behind a resting ball to maintain the ball's location before lifting it.   (3) A tee marker – a pair of objects that define the forward limits of the teeing ground.

MATCH PLAY   One of the two types of golf competition; that in which the reckoning is by holes won, halved, or lost. Each hole played is a distinct contest, and the winner is the side that has won more holes than there remain to be played.

MEDALIST   The player with the lowest score in the qualifying round of a tournament.

NASSAU   A system of scoring based on three points: one point is awarded to the winner of the first nine, one to the winner of the second nine, and one to the winner for the 18 holes.

OBSTRUCTION   Any object erected, placed, or left on the course that is not declared to be an integral part of it.

OUT OF BOUNDS   Identified areas that are not part of the course; therefore, ground on which play is prohibited. A ball is out of bounds when all of it lies off the course.

OUTSIDE AGENCY   Any agency not part of the match. In stroke play, it is any agency not belonging to a competitor's own side.

PAR   The number of strokes assigned to each hole as determined by scores representing expert playing. The cumulative par values for the 18 holes will yield the figure representing par for the course.

PARTNER   A player associated with another on the same side.

PENALTY   A penalty may be loss of hole, one or more strokes added to the score, loss of distance, or disqualification.

PENALTY STROKE   A stroke added to a side's score.

PITCH   A relatively short lofted shot, usually played with a high-numbered iron or wedge.

PROVISIONAL BALL   An additional ball played conditionally on the probability that the original ball played from the same spot may be out of bounds or lost outside a water hazard.

PULL   The flight pattern of a ball traveling in a straight line but off to the left of the target for a right-handed player, or off to the right of the target for a left-handed player.

PUSH   The flight pattern of a ball traveling in a straight line but off to the right of the target for a right-handed player, or off to the left of the target for a left-handed player.

PUTT   To stroke the ball gently and carefully so as to make it roll along the surface of the putting green or some other area. Also the name given to such a stroke.

PUTTING GREEN   The area, especially prepared for putting, that surrounds the hole being played.

ROUGH   Popular term denoting areas of relatively long grass fringing the fairway or adjacent to hazards and greens.

RUB OF THE GREEN   This occurs when a ball in motion is stopped or deflected by an outside agency.

SHAFT   The entire length of a club except its head.

SLICE   The ball's deviation in line of flight by curving to the right of the straight line for a right-handed player, or curving to the left of the straight line for a left-handed player.

SPOON   The club designated as the No. 3 wood.

STANCE   Positioning of the feet when addressing the ball and executing the stroke.

STROKE   The forward movement of the club that is executed with the intention of striking and playing the ball.

STROKE PLAY   One of the two types of golf competition; that in which the winner and subsequent places are determined by accumulation of the total number of strokes scored.

TEEING   When playing from the teeing ground and in accordance with the rules, the ball may be placed on the ground or it may be placed on any substance that will raise it from the ground.

TEEING GROUND   The starting place for the hole to be played. Two markers define the outside limits to the front and sides. The depth is measured by two club lengths from the markers away from the hole.

THROUGH THE GREEN   The whole area of the course except the teeing ground and putting green of the hole being played, and all hazards on the course.

TRACKING   Movement or movements performed during the swing to be in alignment with the intended line of flight.

Equipment

A set of clubs, a supply of golf balls, and a bag to carry them constitutes the player's essential equipment. Convenience has come into the game in the form of motor golf carts to carry players and their bags.

CLUBS

There are two general types of golf club: woods and irons (see Figs. 4.2 and 4.3). A player in an official tournament is limited by rule to a maximum of fourteen clubs while playing a round. The set of fourteen usually consists of four woods, nine irons and a putter. The beginner, however, does not need so many clubs. He will find two woods (a driver and a spoon), four irons (3, 5, 7, 9), and a putter adequate when first learning.

Woods have clubheads of wood, and irons have clubheads of iron. Clubs also vary in the loft of the clubface and length of the shaft. Among the woods, the loft is least with the driver, No. 1, 11°, and gradually increases with the brassie, No. 2, 14°, the spoon, No. 3,

17º, and the No. 4 wood, 20º. Among the irons, the loft is least with the No. 1 iron, 19º, and increases as follows: No. 2, 23º, No. 3, 27º, No. 4, 31º, No. 5, 35º, No. 6, 39º, No. 7, 43º, and No. 9, 51º. The loft is greatest with the wedge, 55º. Thus, the range in loft varies from near perpendicular (No. 1 wood) to as much as 55º with the wedge. As loft increases, the shaft length decreases, usually by steps of approximately half an inch every two clubs, with the exception of the brassie, which commonly comes in the same length as the driver. The standard length of the driver is 43" for men. The standard length of the No. 2 iron is 38½" for men. Women's clubs run approximately one inch shorter than men's. When placing special orders with the manufacturer, specifications for each club may be prescribed to suit the individual's idiosyncrasies.

The putter is in a class all its own; it is the shortest club in the set and has little or no loft. Most putters have iron heads, but some have wood heads.

The beginner often is perplexed by this great array of clubs but with a little playing experience on the golf course, he realizes why there are long clubs and short ones. He realizes that

Figure 4.1   Motor carts with equipment.

there are clubs to keep the ball low and clubs to raise the ball. Later, as he becomes more skillful, he appreciates the clubs that play the ball so that it continues to roll for some distance after it lands, and the clubs that play so that the ball bites, or comes to an abrupt halt, upon landing. He needs these because of the wide variety in terrain, which include bare surfaces, smooth or rough grass, deep patches, sand bunkers, trees, water hazards, and so on. Virtually every shot provides a different condition of play.

It would be misleading to offer a standard of distances set and scaled to each club, because each player acquires his own range of playing distances, based on his own ability. For each one of his clubs, each player gets to know his own limitations in the use of the club and plays accordingly. Indeed, experience over several years of diligent learning will prove to be the best guide. However, the chart on the next page will be helpful to the beginner in learning about clubs and their relationship to distances.

The average distances on the next page do not take into account adverse wind conditions. Heavy winds will alter these distances somewhat.

Figure 4.2   Clubhead (wood).

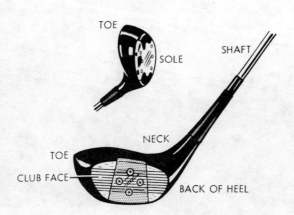

Club	Carry: Strong Players	Carry: Average Players
Driver	240 yards	190 yards
Brassie	230 yards	180 yards
Spoon	220 yards	170 yards
4 wood	210 yards	160 yards
5 wood	200 yards	150 yards
1 iron	200 yards	160 yards
2 iron	190 yards	150 yards
3 iron	180 yards	140 yards
4 iron	170 yards	130 yards
5 iron	160 yards	120 yards
6 iron	150 yards	110 yards
7 iron	140 yards	100 yards
8 iron	130 yards	90 yards
9 iron	120 yards	80 yards
Wedge	110 yards	70 yards

Invariably, as a golfer gains greater proficiency, he will wonder if he could not improve still more. If he is convinced that he possesses a reliable swing and that he executes his shots well, but they somehow just do not come off well, he solicitously looks to his clubs and his golf balls. He wonders whether he can find something about them that might be improved.

Figure 4.3   Set of irons.

First, he needs to understand the structure of the club. Golf clubs are built scientifically to suit certain physical characteristics of the player. Aside from the length of the shaft and the loft of the clubface, the flexibility of the shaft and the weight of the head are variables in the structure of a club. These latter two variables are "matched," and the result of any match is known as the swing weight of a club or of a set of clubs. Swing weights are designated by symbols consisting of a letter and numeral. For example, C−8 would represent a light swing weight as compared to D−9 or E−0, which would represent heavy swing weights. Flexibility of the shaft is generally represented by the letters L, A, R, S, and XS, ranging from very soft or flexible to extra stiff, respectively. Thus, the weight concentrated at the clubhead and the flexibility characteristic of the shaft can provide an assortment of combinations. The determining factor is the individual's physical ability as represented by the strength and speed of movement of his hands and arms. Consultation with a competent professional is recommended for the best fitting of clubs to one's needs.

THE BALL

It is important to note not only the standards of size and weight set by rule, but also a ball's compression rating. The strong-hitting golfer, for instance, should play with a high-

Figure 4.4   Putters.

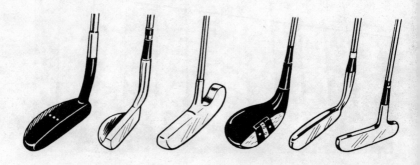

compression ball, and the soft swinger should use a ball with a relatively lower compression rating (see Fig. 4.5). Compression ratings are indicated by numerals. For example, a high-compression ball would be indicated by 100. Thus, the strong hitter will get best results with the high-compression ball. The soft hitter will be wise to use a ball with a rating of about 80.

The dimples and surface conditon of the ball are also important to consider. The function of the dimples is to take hold of the opposing air and to spin it around the ball while the ball is in flight. Since higher pressure builds up below, the ball rises to the area of least resistance. When well hit, the trajectory and carry of the ball will be drastically effected if the dimples of the ball are worn or damaged. A ball worn as much as .002 inches would show an erratic flight pattern of rises and dips. After approximately 75 to 100 full shots this would result. Hence, the serious golfer uses a ball with a compression rating suited to his manner of play, and avoids using one that has been worn or damaged.

Figure 4.5 Compression of a golf ball at impact.

Photo courtesy of Dr. H. E. Edgerton (MIT).

Golf
Etiquette

The first thing any beginning golfer should learn is the code of etiquette. Etiquette involves the behavior on the course of all players at all times, as well as involving the physical elements of the course itself. A careful analysis of the basic components of etiquette will make it quite clear that it is vital to the ultimate enjoyment of golf.

It should be noted that although etiquette occupies Section I of the Rules of Golf and includes nine basic statements, that section, unlike Section III, which deals with the rules of play, invokes no penalties as such. It is therefore incumbent upon the individual to observe the tenets of etiquette:

1. Avoid making any sound or movement that might distract another player preparatory to and during execution of a stroke. A player wants to have no distractions when he is concentrating upon playing a stroke. Such a simple act as standing directly behind a player within his field of vision could be distracting.

2. Watch the honor on the teeing ground. Other players should not tee their balls until the player having the honor has played his first stroke.

3. Never play a stroke until all other players in view are clearly out of range. One of the greatest dangers and nuisances is to have golf balls flying indiscriminately over the course. A ball in flight can inflict grave injuries. Extra care must be taken in areas where there are hidden valleys, dog-legs, and other terrain causing restricted view of the area of play. If necessary, the customary warning cry "Fore!" should be shouted in the direction of unsuspecting players if the ball appears to be headed in their direction. Sometimes, doing this prior to playing the ball will avoid an unhappy accident.

4. Learn to play at a normal pace without causing undue delay. If you ever have played behind extremely slow players, you undoubtedly have been exasperated to the point of not enjoying your game. Golf can be slow enough while simply waiting for the player whose ball is away to play first. Everyone should make a sincere effort to be ready to execute his stroke when his turn comes. Do not take extra practice swings while others are waiting for you to play your shot. And do not take too much time making up your mind what club to select. Be considerate of those behind you.

5. Do not oblige others to wait while you search for a lost ball. When a player must search for his ball, the other players should assist him. But if another group of players is following close behind, the searching party should signal to them to pass.

6. After completing your play from a sand bunker, leave the bunker in order by carefully leveling out all impressions and holes you have made. Use the rakes or similar implements placed nearby for this purpose. If no tools are available, use your clubhead and do the best you can. Most golfers do not relish playing out of a sand bunker, let alone having to play a shot where the ball

not only is embedded in sand but also lies in someone else's footprint.

7. Replace any divot you have made, and press it into the ground. "REPLACE DIVOT" may be a common sign on the golf course. The players must do their share in helping to keep the golf course in the best possible condition. It aids the players behind not to have to find their ball at rest in someone's divot scars. This care for the course also applies to the putting green. Any damage made by your ball to the putting green surface should be carefully repaired before you leave the green. This can be done nicely with the sharp point of a golf tee.

8. Take all possible measures for proper care of the putting green. While walking on the green do not drag your shoes. Do not drop your clubs on the green surface, since such actions can damage it. Be careful of the green when handling the flagstick. When replacing the flagstick—remember always to do so before leaving the green—be especially careful not to damage the lip of the hole. Place the flagstick in the center of the hole with utmost care.

9. Leave the putting green immediately after completing your play of the hole. Occasionally, players cannot remember clearly how many strokes were played and find themselves, in a moment of despair, on the putting green recounting the shots. If players are in the back and ready to play when you are through putting but still remain on the putting green recounting your strokes, you will annoy them, to say the least. Also, consider a precaution that will facilitate your exit from the area of the putting green; when you are going to the putting green following your approach shot, leave your golf bag on the side of the green nearest the next tee or the clubhouse, as the case may be. You will thus get out of the way much faster and more courteously. By all means, avoid ever leaving your golf bag around the approach to the green.

Now you can see how etiquette, when properly observed, makes golf safer, keeps the course in the best possible playing condition at all times, and enhances opportunity for greater enjoyment by all players.

Rules
of
Golf

6

Golf rules appear complicated to the experienced player as well as to the uninitiated or beginner. This is because the rules cover every possible contingency of organization, competition, player status and behavior, and a myriad of circumstances that go into the conduct of the game on a universal and world-wide scale. The rules of golf as approved by the United States Golf Association and the Royal and Ancient Golf Club of St. Andrews, Scotland, are the official and world-accepted rules for the game. Every player should have the current copy of the rules book published by the USGA.

The rules book is divided into three sections, dealing, respectively, with etiquette, definitions, and the rules of play. This chapter will concentrate upon the rules of play.

There are 41 rules of play. The beginner undoubtedly will be overwhelmed by the complexity of technical details. Rules are inextricably intertwined with definitions and terminology. Therefore, patience in learning is necessary in order to understand the rules and apply them correctly. The score turned in by a player may not be absolutely correct if he does not know the rules thoroughly. For such knowledge, there can be no short cut, but only conscientious study of every rule in every possible detail. Obviously, this would take considerable time and cannot be done in this book. Instead, this chapter offers a look at the essentials of the most common situations the average player will encounter in a round of play. Thus, our order of discussion will follow the probable order of actual play. At the end of the chapter is a list of questions intended to help the student determine whether he knows the material correctly.

PRELIMINARY INFORMATION

There are two types of competition: match play and stroke play (see Chapter 3). One of the major distinctions is in the method of determining the winner. In match play it is by holes won, halved, or lost. In stroke play it is by total strokes scored. Another major distinction is the general penalty system. Unless otherwise provided for in the rules, the penalty for breach of a rule is loss of hole (in match play), or two strokes (in stroke play).

In an official tournament, a player may carry no more than 14 clubs when starting a stipulated round.

The ball and the clubs must conform to official specifications.

A second ball may be played in stroke play only—when a competitor is doubtful of his rights or of the procedure. He must then play out both his original ball and his second ball.

Every breach of the rules entails the enforcement of a penalty. It may be a one-stroke, two-stroke, loss-of-hole, stroke-and-distance penalty, or disqualification, according to the particular rule. Until one unmistakably knows the rules, it is best to look up the relevant rule whenever a penalty is assessed.

STARTING PLAY

The ball must be played from within the limits of the teeing ground. In match play, this is subject to the discretion of the player's opponent. In stroke play, the player must play from within the teeing ground. It should be noted that a player may take his stance outside the teeing ground in order to play a ball within it.

A player knocking a ball not in play off the tee in addressing it may re-tee it without penalty. When a player has made a stroke, the stroke must be counted whether the ball be moving or not, and no penalty is incurred.

PLAYING THROUGH THE GREEN

The rules covering this portion of play include Rules 16 to 33.

When the ball is played from the teeing ground, it (1) goes out of bounds or (2) remains in bounds. If it goes out of bounds, the player may play a provisional ball, in accordance with Rule 30. The penalty for a ball out of bounds is the stroke-and-distance penalty. If the ball remains in bounds, one of the following must be decided: (1) the ball is playable or unplayable or (2) the ball is lost. The player is the sole judge as to whether his ball is unplayable. If he declares his ball unplayable, he has these options: (1) to apply the stroke-and-distance penalty or (2), under a one-stroke penalty, to drop a ball within two clublengths or behind the point where the ball lay, but with no limit as to the distance behind. If the player declares his ball lost, the procedure and the penalty are the same as for a ball out of bounds.

Generally, the ball must be played as it lies (Rule 16). A player may not improve his line of play or the position of his ball by moving, bending or breaking anything fixed or growing. Neither may he improve the lie of his ball (Rule 17).

Any loose impediment may be removed except when both the impediment and the ball lie in, or touch, a hazard (Rule 18).

In the execution of a stroke, the ball must be struck with the head of the club. The stroke must not be a pushing, scraping, or spooning of the ball (Rule 19).

When a player has played a stroke with a ball other than his own in match play (except in a hazard) he loses the hole. In stroke play, if he plays a stroke or strokes with a ball other than his own (except in a hazard), he must find his own ball and then play it, adding two penalty strokes to his score for the hole. Strokes played by a competitor with the wrong ball do not count on the player's score. The player is disqualified if he does not rectify his mistake (Rule 21).

Under certain circumstances covered by the rules, a player may lift his ball and drop it—facing the hole, standing erect, and dropping the ball behind him over his shoulder (Rule 22). Under certain conditions, a player may clean his ball. They include unplayable lie, relief from an obstruction, a ball lifted from casual water, ground under repair, a water hazard, and on the putting green (Rule 23).

The ball must not be played while it is moving. Exceptions include a ball falling off the tee, striking the ball twice, and a ball in water. The penalty for breach of this rule (No. 25) is loss of hole (in match play) or two strokes (in stroke play).

When a ball at rest is moved by an outside agency, it must be replaced without penalty. When the player accidentally moves a ball at rest, he must incur a penalty stroke, and the ball must be played as it lies (Rule 27).

Any movable obstruction may be removed. When a ball lies on, or touches, an immovable obstruction, relief is permitted. This also applies when an immovable obstruction is within two clublengths of the ball and there is interference with the player's play. Relief permits lifting and dropping within two clublengths of that point on the outside of the obstruction which is nearest the ball (Rule 31). Relief is permitted also when a ball lies in or touches casual water, on ground under repair, or in a hole, cast, or runway made by a burrowing animal, reptile or bird. The player may then lift and drop as near as possible to the spot of the ball affording maximum relief, but not nearer the hole. If a ball in a hazard is dropped in the hazard, there is no penalty. If it is dropped outside the hazard, there is a penalty of one stroke (Rule 32). The hazard and water hazard rule (Rule 33) is quite involved. The following general points must be observed:

> When a ball lies in a hazard, the player may not touch the ground, sand, or water with a club or otherwise, nor touch or move a loose impediment lying in or touching the hazard, nor test the condition of the hazard. The player may place his feet firmly in taking his stance. He is entitled to relief from obstructions. He may remove as much sand, fallen leaves, or the like as will enable him to see the top of the ball. The ball, however, may not be lifted for identification.

REVIEW QUESTIONS

It is recommended that an official rules book be used in seeking answers to the questions below. Answers to most of them are provided in this chapter, but the actual experience of searching in the rules book in relation to a stated situation is a worthwhile exercise and promotes familiarity with the book.

> What club or clubs may a player use—on the teeing ground, in a hazard, on the putting green, through the green? What is the maximum number of clubs a player may carry, and how may he replace or add a club? (Rules 2, 3)

> What is the difference between match play and stroke play? What constitutes advice, and what are breaches of this rule? Who may give advice? Who may receive advice? (Rules 6, 7, 9, 10)

> What is a second ball, and what are the restrictions upon its use? (Rule 11)

> What differences are there between match play and stroke play when a player plays his first ball from outside the teeing ground? When may a player re-tee his ball if it falls

off the tee? In relation to this, when does he count a stroke? (Rules 13, 14)

What constitutes touching or moving the ball purposely as contrasted to moving it accidentally? What penalties are involved? (Rule 16)

When is a player permitted to improve the position or lie of the ball, and under what restrictions? (Rule 17)

What differences exist in the loose-impediment rule when applied (1) through the green, (2) in a hazard, or (3) on the putting green? (Rule 18)

What explicit restrictions are there concerning the contact of the ball and the clubhead in the play of a stroke? (Rule 19)

What differences are there between match play and stroke play when a player plays a wrong ball (1) through the green or (2) from a hazard? If you inadvertently play your opponent's ball from the rough bordering the fairway, what is the correct ruling? If you inadvertently play your fellow competitor's ball from the sand bunker onto the green and immediately discover this fact, what is the correct ruling? If both you and your opponent finish the play of a hole with identical scores, but you realize that you have exchanged balls sometime in the play of the hole, what is the correct ruling? (Rule 21)

What is the correct ruling in the case of a player's ball in motion being deflected by his bag or golf clubs? What is the correct ruling when a player's ball in motion is deflected by his opponent? (Rule 26)

What is an outside agency, and what is the correct ruling when a ball at rest is moved by an outside agency—(1) in match play and (2) in stroke play? What is the penalty or correct ruling if a caddie accidentally moves his player's ball while the ball is at rest? (Rule 27)

What is the penalty for a ball lost outside a water hazard? What is the penalty for a ball's having gone out of bounds?

What are the penalty and the options for a ball declared unplayable? When may a player play a provisional ball? How many times may one play a provisional ball during the play of a hole? During the play of a round? During the play of a tournament? (Rules 29, 30)

What are obstructions, and how do they differ from loose impediments? What relief may a player have with regard to obstructions? Where are movable obstructions found? Where are immovable obstructions found? (Rule 31)

If your ball lies in casual water in a sand bunker, what relief, if any, may you have, and what constitute possible breaches of this rule? What is the procedure for lifting and dropping a ball in ground under repair? (Rule 32)

When your ball lies completely buried in a sand bunker, what may you do to improve your situation? When your ball lies partially covered by leaves in a sand bunker, what may you do to improve your situation? What are the options for a ball lost in a water hazard? What are the options for a ball declared unplayable in a water hazard? (Rule 33)

What are the correct rulings for a ball played out of turn on the putting green when (1) the ball drops into the hole, and (2) the ball is not holed out? What is the correct ruling when your ball lies in a sand bunker two yards from the green and your stroke causes it to strike the flagstick attended. When a player uses his putter to press down spike marks on the surface of the putting green in the line of his putt between his ball and the hole? When a ball played on the putting green is stopped or deflected by an outside agency? May a player make a stroke on the putting green from a stance astride the line of putt without penalty? (Rules 34, 35)

Executing the Full Swing

7

In an activity such as golf, in which body and hands are actively used in swinging a club while the feet are in a stationary position, efficient coordination depends upon how well the body works in harmony with the hands, how well each hand works in harmony with the other, and how well total balance is maintained over the feet. Generally, discussion of golf skill and technique focuses upon three main elements: the grip, the stance, and the execution. The execution is commonly referred to as the swing. In this book, the term *execution* will refer to the action that causes the swing of the clubhead, while the term *swing* will be used as a description of the execution.

THE GRIP

A good grip is important in bringing about harmonious action of the hands. Since one hand is positioned above the other on the grip, or handle, of the club, a mechanical couple exists—that is, a pair of equal parallel forces acting in opposite directions and tending to produce rotation. For the right-handed player, the left hand is positioned above the right hand. Thus, the hand on top has the primary function of control and of leading the movement of the clubhead, while the lower hand has the function of supplying the power through the clubhead in its work of striking the ball. It is important to remember in grasping the grip, that the fingers uphold it; the palms do not press down on it. The following steps should be used in placing the hands on the grip:

1. Place the clubhead on the ground, and put the upper hand (left hand for right-handed players, right hand for left-handed players) to the grip in the manner shown in Fig. 7.1. Locate the grip as far toward the tips of the fingers as possible. Make sure that the palm is facing away from the ball's target and that the back of the hand gives the impression of aligning itself with the clubface, which itself should be aligned squarely with the target.

2. Complete the upper-hand grip by closing the hand in such a way as to position the thumb downward along the grip slightly inside (away from the target) the midline of the shaft. The index finger should hook around the shaft in an attempt to point back toward the thumb. In this upper-hand grasp, it is important to feel the pressure being exerted in the little fingers.

Figure 7.1   Placing upper hand on grip: Steps 1, 2, and 3.

3. Place the lower hand to the grip as shown in Fig. 7.2. Again it should be noted that the grip is held in the fingers. The palm is positioned to the inside of the shaft, resting over the extended thumb of the upper hand. The little finger of the lower hand is placed over the index finger of the upper hand, forming an overlap—giving its name to this manner of gripping, that is, the overlap grip. The overlap grip is used by most professionals and top-ranking amateurs. The rationale commonly given is that this provides the most appropriate harmonious working relationship between the two hands.

The hands should be trained to work together as one. Though the grip should be firm, with the pressure exerted in the fingers, it should not be so tight as to render the wrists immobile or stiff. The wrists should be allowed complete freedom of movement. Constantly check to see that the face of the club is square to the target in addressing the ball.

Though the overlap grip is preferred by most golfers, two other grips are used. The main difference is in the relationship of the little finger of the lower hand to the index finger of the upper hand. Figure 7.3 shows two views of the overlap grip in which the little finger of the lower hand overlaps the index

Figure 7.2   Placing lower hand on grip: Steps 1 and 2.

finger of the upper hand. Figure 7.4 shows two views of the so-called ten-finger, or natural, grip. Figure 7.5 shows the interlocking grip, in which the little finger of the lower hand interlocks with the index finger of the upper hand, displacing the little finger of the upper hand from the grip.

THE STANCE

The stance is the positioning of the player's feet. It serves two main purposes: (1) to provide the player with the means of aligning himself with the target in relation to the ball and of determining how he wants his body and hands to perform, and (2) to provide the foundation upon which the stability of the execution and the player's sense of balance are maintained. Thus, when the player addresses the ball, he places much of his confidence in his execution in the manner of his stance. Every player eventually develops his own pattern or sequence of movements in arriving at this stance for each shot. Generally, the pattern involves these basic maneuvers: (1) selecting the club, (2) picking the club from the bag, (3) tentatively gripping the club and approaching the ball, (4) mentally drawing a flight pattern for the shot, (5) stepping up to the ball or near to the ball and taking one or more practice swings, and (6) taking the stance. In taking the stance, some players

Figure 7.3   Overlap grip.

approach the ball by bringing both feet close together in line with, and at the desired distance from, the ball. Then they proceed to move the feet apart, with preference to moving one foot—usually the same foot first—and then following with the other. Some players first place in the desired position in relation to the ball the foot that is nearer the target. Others prefer to place the foot that is farther from the target first. Whatever the pattern of addressing the ball in taking the stance, the stance itself will take one of three basic forms: (1) the square, or parallel, stance (Fig. 7.6), (2) the open stance (Fig. 7.7), and (3) the closed stance (Fig. 7.8).

The essential differences among these forms of stance are found in the relationship of the feet to the flight line (assuming that the flight line is a straight line from the ball to the target). When both feet are equally distant from the flight line, we say that the stance line is parallel with the flight line—thus the *parallel stance*. Players more popularly refer to this as the square stance. When the foot that is nearer the target is positioned farther away from the flight line than the foot that is farther from the target, we say that the stance is open to the target—thus the *open stance*. When the foot that is nearer the target is positioned closer to the flight line than the foot that is farther from the target, we say that the stance is closed to the target—thus the *closed stance*. Generally, it is recommended

Figure 7.4   Ten-finger grip.

that players use the parallel stance for most of their shots. The advantage is in keeping the body entirely oriented within a frame of reference that is parallel and square to the flight line. The advantage in the closed stance is that it permits a greater amount of trunk (upper body) and hip rotation in the backswing. This allows greater application of force, resulting in more potential power. It is not uncommon to find players using the closed stance in driving off the teeing ground. The advantage in the open stance is chiefly the restriction it puts upon the backswing, thus giving the player potentially better control, primarily in lofting the ball when using the shorter clubs. It should be pointed out, however, that the stances other than the parallel stance will permit greater deviation from the flight line in the path of the clubhead during the backswing and forward movement of the clubhead. Some of the problems related to this are pointed out and discussed in Chapter 9.

Figure 7.5   Interlocking grip.

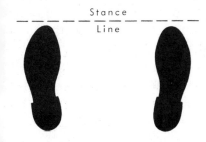

Figure 7.6   Parallel stance.

Figure 7.7   Open stance.

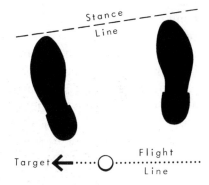

Figure 7.8   Closed stance.

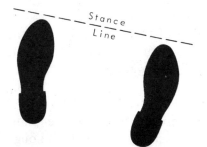

EXECUTION

The term *swing* has become the key word in the language of golf, because it represents what is perhaps the most critical concept in all the physical aspects of the game. The word *swing* taken by itself is not clearly understood, because the most common assumption is that it refers to swinging the club— vaguely the entire club. Instead, one should conceive of the execution of the golf swing as swinging the clubhead. It makes all the difference in the world when one attempts to swing the whole club in contrast to swinging the clubhead. Swinging the entire club invariably involves pulling at the handle of the club and then, at some instant, lunging or nudging at the ball with the clubhead. This results in an uneven flow of energy, with spurts of jerky movements throughout the swing. Swinging the clubhead, however, takes into account the fact that the head moves over a greater distance, and thus at a greater velocity, than the handle. This means that the hands, working at the handle, must direct their work to the clubhead. Of course, this task is more difficult with a long-shafted club such as the driver than with a short-shafted club such as the No. 9 iron. It cannot be emphasized enough that the hands play a vital role in executing the swing. In particular, the lead hand, positioned above the lower hand, functions significantly in controlling the movement of the clubhead. The lower hand follows in an integrated pattern and supplies the major force, imparting power through the impact of the clubhead upon the ball. The rest of the body aids in supplying additional power, and it must coordinate with the hands in executing the proper movement to bring about the effective swinging of the clubhead.

Let us analyze the execution of the full swing, using the drive as an example. At the address position, preparatory to the initial movement of the clubhead backward, the arms form a full extension to the grip, with the shaft of the club projecting this extension downward to the clubhead (Fig. 7.9). The general posture is nearly erect, with no conscious rigidity in the joints. The player's head should be kept as steady as possible, though not absolutely still, throughout the execution of the swing. This positioning of the head is maintained in relation to the position of the ball. The dominating action in the initial movement of the clubhead backward in its takeback is performed by the upper hand, since it is the upper hand that dominates and controls the movement of the clubhead through the entire path of the backswing (Fig. 7.10). In a continuous action, the knee nearer the target begins to flex and turn inward, literally following the clubhead. The left-shoulder movement is executed much in the same manner—turning in relation to the movement of the clubhead backward and upward. Figure 7.10 shows the backswing nearly completed to the top. Other key points to be aware of are these:

The lead arm is kept as straight as possible at the elbow to ensure maximum leverage in extending the club.

The knee farther from the target is kept slightly flexed to ensure the best possible rotation of the hips in the direction of the movement of the clubhead backward and upward.

Figure 7.9   Drive: Addressing the ball.

The heel on the lead side is raised slightly off the ground. A minimum of raising is recommended — on no account more than 3" — to ensure balance.

The heel on the side farther from the target remains on the ground throughout the backswing.

When first learning the proper execution of the full swing, the golfer should make a conscious effort briefly to maintain the position at the top of the backswing—a slight pause. This has been found helpful by many beginners, and by advanced players also, in ensuring proper alignment of the clubhead before starting it on its movement downward. The pause provides a better sense of control and inhibits any attempt to rush the clubhead back to the ball.

The initial action of the clubhead's downward movement involves lowering the lead hand in an attempt to get the mass of the clubhead moving downward. In a continuous action, the knee and hip on the lead side begin to track slightly backward, and the lead shoulder begins to turn toward the target in a rotation that is more upward than backward. The execution of the clubhead's movement should be a swinging and tracking motion, and all temptation to move it with a lunge or to rush it to the ball by forcing at the grip should be avoided. Figure 7.11 shows the execution of the swing downward from the top of the backswing to the point where the clubhead is nearing the ball. It is

Figure 7.10 Drive: Initiating movement backward through top of backswing.

important both to keep the player's head as steady as possible and also to concentrate upon keeping the lead arm as straight as possible. At the same time, it is important not to allow the knee on the far side to lock into a straight position; it should bend in coordination with the movement of the clubhead toward the ball. Just before the impact, the lower hand smoothly comes into action, supplying the extra power to direct the clubhead to the ball. The key to the action at this stage is to execute the hand action so as to track the clubhead through the intended flight line in a continuous movement toward the target. The action should not be simply forcing the clubhead at the ball. The follow-through action must maintain a full extension of the arms until the momentum of the clubhead in its arc upward begins to cause the wrists and elbows to bend toward the player's head, with the hands finishing high above his head and shoulders (Fig. 7.12). There should be a conscious attempt to track the movement of the clubhead in the flight line and in plane to the target throughout the downward movement of the clubhead, the forward movement, and the follow-through. Other key points to watch are:

> At impact, the hands should be in direct alignment – that is, a straight line from the ball, through the grip, and up through the lead arm, so that the lower hand is directly beneath the upper hand in this line (Fig. 7.11).

Figure 7.11   Drive: Clubhead movement downward nearing impact.

The player's attention should be on the ball, with a track — the intended flight line — extending through the ball to some point in front of the ball along the ground and projected toward the target, this line directs the hands in tracking the clubhead (Fig. 7.12).

The heel on the lead side should be planted firmly on the ground.

The heel on the far side should come off the ground, during the clubhead movement, in coordination with the movement of the knee on that same side. The movement of the knee should be toward the ball.

Stroboscopic photographs of the drive, both at 120 pictures per second, are shown in Fig. 7.13. Many of the points discussed here may be observed in these photographs. Note particularly the squareness of the clubface through impact.

The execution of the full swing is basically the same with the other clubs as with the driver. Figures 7.14 through 7.32 show this for the 3-wood swing, the 5-wood swing, the 2-iron swing, the 5-iron swing, and the 8-iron swing. These are all full-swing executions. The sense of timing in the execution varies from club to club due to the differences in the lengths of the clubs.

Figure 7.12 Drive: Movement forward after impact through finish position.

Figure 7.13   Stroboscopic photograph of a golf drive.

Photos curtesy of Dr. H. E. Edgerton (MIT)

Figure 7.14   Addressing ball with 3-wood.

Figure 7.15   Clubhead (3-wood) initiating movement backward through top of backswing.

Figure 7.16   3-wood in downward movement nearing impact.

Figure 7.17   3-wood in forward movement after impact through finish position.

Figure 7.18 5-wood: Addressing the ball.

Figure 7.19 5-wood: Initiating clubhead movement backward through top of swing.

Figure 7.20 5-wood in downward movement nearing impact.

Figure 7.21 5-wood in forward movement after impact through finish position.

Figure 7.22 2-Iron: Addressing the ball.

Figure 7.23 2-Iron: Initiating clubhead movement backward through top of backswing position.

Figure 7.24 2-Iron: Clubhead in downward movement through finish position of full swing.

Figure 7.25   5-Iron: Addressing the ball.

Figure 7.26   5-Iron: Initiating clubhead movement backward through top of backswing.

Figure 7.27 5-Iron: Clubhead in downward movement through near impact with the ball.

Figure 7.28 5-Iron: Clubhead movement forward after impact through finish position of full swing.

Figure 7.29   8-Iron: Addressing the ball.

Figure 7.30   8-Iron: Initiating clubhead movement backward through top of backswing.

Figure 7.31   8-Iron: Clubhead in downward movement through near impact with the ball.

Figure 7.32   8-Iron: Clubhead movement forward after impact through finish position of full swing.

REVIEW QUESTIONS

Is your hand grip firm but not rigid?

The grip is essentially an action in which the fingers hold the handle of the club. Grip firmly by concentrating effort on the little, ring, and middle fingers of the upper hand and on the thumb and index finger of the lower hand.

Is your grip at the top of the backswing firm?

Remember the fingers at the top of the backswing; do not allow the lead hand to loosen its grip on the handle.

Have you developed a sound lead-arm and hand movement?

Maintain a straight lead-arm elbow throughout the backswing and on through impact without tightening at the wrist. Freedom in wrist movement is essential for control of the clubhead and for application of force at impact.

Is the clubhead kept square and on track to the target at impact? Does the ball travel in a straight line of flight?

Turning the clubface causes deviations from the straight line in the flight pattern of the ball. Hence, the clubface must be kept square and on track to the target throughout impact. The lower hand should be as nearly as possible directly beneath the upper hand and in a straight line of the ball at the moment of impact.

Are you keeping the clubhead on track to the target through impact as long as possible?

In addition to keeping the clubface square, the movement of the clubhead must travel on track to the target through impact as long as possible. Keeping both arms straight in extending the arms and the club toward the target is important. Do not just rush the clubhead at the ball and then attempt to scoop up the ball. The key point to remember is proper leverage performance.

Is your knee action coordinated?

The movements of the knees must be coordinated with the movement of the clubhead. On the backswing, the knee on the lead side turns, and the knee on the far side remains slightly flexed. On the downward movement of the clubhead and through the forward swing, the knee on the far side, following the clubhead, turns while the knee on the lead side tracks slightly backward.

Is your stance stable and are you in balance?

Stability and balance are related to the movement of the clubhead. Attempts to rush the swing of the clubhead will result in jerky movements that will throw the golfer off balance. Unnecessary movements of the player's head contribute also to loss of control in executing the swing of the clubhead and will result in throwing the golfer off balance.

Basic Complementary Strokes

The basic full swing described and discussed in Chapter 7 is essential for driving off the teeing ground and playing the ball through the green, covering as much distance in as few strokes as possible. The shots of the basic full swing variety account for 25 to 35 per cent of the strokes that go on the score card. The remainder comes from the attempts to approach and to get onto the green and then into the hole. Usually, the player takes an average of no less than two strokes on the putting green. Thus, the "scoring game" depends upon the golfer's proficiency in these basic complementary strokes. A sound approach and a good putting game help to reduce his score by many strokes. Diligent study and practice of these strokes are absolutely essential to a sound scoring game.

THE PUTT

The putt is the least complex stroke; yet players often dread it enough to freeze on a short putt. Perhaps the fact that greens are not all alike adds to the uncertainty in putting. They vary in speed, in type of grass, in slope, and in degree of undulation. The key to good putting is confidence, which comes only with success in developing a sound putting stroke—the result of lots and lots of putting practice. Since par is computed on the basis of allowing two putts on the green, the good golfer realizes that he cannot afford to be careless when executing the first putt. Strict attention to the first putt is perhaps the most demanding act of concentration in playing a hole. Of course, possessing a sound and confident stroke makes it much easier to concentrate.

Individuality is most evident in putting. Styles vary so widely that clubs used in putting come in every imaginable shape. Every golfer has his own preference as to type of putter and style of putting. Nevertheless, there are some fundamental points that are essential to good putting.

The Grip

The putting grip differs slightly from the regular, or overlap, grip. The hands are placed so that they face each other with the thumbs of both hands aligned with the downward line of the shaft. The club's grip is held in the palms of both hands. The overlapping is done by extending the index finger of the upper hand downward over the last two fingers of the lower hand. This is commonly referred to as the reverse overlap grip (Fig. 8.1).

Figure 8.1   Putting grip: Reverse overlap.

The Stance

Addressing the ball and taking the stance are determined relative to squaring with the line of putt. The clubface is addressed to the ball at right angles to the line of putt. The positions of shoulders, hips, and stance line are parallel to the line of putt. (Some players, however, prefer to assume a slightly open stance.) The head should be held steady and as directly over the ball as possible. Although the player's distance from the ball should be a comfortable one, most golfers prefer to stand as close to the ball as that will permit. The distribution of weight also should be comfortable. The hands should be kept as close to the thighs as possible (Fig. 8.2).

The Stroke

There are two common methods of stroking the putt: (1) the pendulum stroke, with almost no breaking of the wrists, allowing an extended follow-through, with the pendulum of the stroke fixed at the shoulders; (2) a crisp tapping stroke with noticeable wrist action and comparatively less follow-through. Each player must select his own method in accordance with his

Figure 8.2   Putting stance.

experience. But in any case, the following basic points must be kept in mind at all times:

There are two problems in putting: distance and direction. One way to regulate distance is to control the length of the takeback. Keeping the putter face squared to the line of putt insures direction.

Keep the putter head as close to the surface of the green as possible throughout the entire stroke. Lifting the putter head contributes to irregular turning or twisting of it, which invariably causes gyrations in the roll of the ball. The ball should roll with a true vertical overspin in the direction of the hole.

The player's body and head remain as motionless as possible throughout the stroke.

The entire stroke is deliberate and unrushed. The takeback movement should be smooth and slow. The forward movement is made in the same tempo as the takeback, without any attempt to accelerate as the putter head approaches the ball.

Sensitivity or "touch" in putting is acquired by developing awareness of the action of the thumb and index finger of the lower hand. These two fingers essentially control the feel of the action applied to the putter head.

Figure 8.3 Putting: Addressing the ball.

The player should develop a consistent pattern in lining up the putt, reading the green for speed and slope or break, addressing the ball, sticking to the original judgment of distance and determination of direction, and stroking with confidence.

Note: Putting essentially involves correct distance and direction.

Figure 8.4 Putting: Initiating of takeback through finish of stroke.

THE CHIP SHOT

Frequently, golfers believe that good chipping goes with good putting, since good chipping consistently places the ball near enough to the hole to take the pressure off the putting. The chip is essentially a *run-up* shot. It travels in a low trajectory and is aimed at a predetermined spot—preferably on the surface of the green—calculated to allow the ball to take the necessary roll to the hole. Whenever possible—that is, whenever the approach to the green is fairly level and there are no bunkers or other hazards to play over—the chip shot gives the best percentage in getting the ball near enough to the hole for a one-putt chance of holing out. Usually, the chip is executed from about 20 yards or less off the green. It is worth every golfer's spare time to work on chipping as a means of cutting down the number of strokes it takes to get near the hole.

Club Selection

Two problems are involved in deciding on the club for a chip shot: (1) where is the best spot for the ball to land; and (2) how fast is the green and how far must the ball roll to the hole: Answering these questions gives a better idea of which

Figure 8.5 Chip shot: Addressing the ball.

club can serve best under the conditions. Generally, the more lofted the clubface, the greater the margin of contact error between the clubface and the ball. Therefore, the least lofted club should be preferred. Players get into the habit of automatically relying upon one or two clubs for all of their chip shots. This works as long as the conditions of play do not vary much. It would be better in the long run to be able to play chip shots with as many different clubs as possible, to enable you to play different conditions as you face them. As in putting, the important thing is confidence—a reward of experience and practice.

The Grip

The grip for the chip shot does not vary from the one used in regular shots of the full swing variety. Many players, however, prefer to grip the club farther down on the handle, because experience shows that this improves control and increases accuracy.

The Stance

The open stance is recommended for the chip shot. Since the distance the clubhead travels in the takeback is relatively short, the feet are positioned closer together than in the full swing. The shot usually calls for a low trajectory and considerable rolling of the ball. Thus, the stance is taken with the ball in a line off the forward foot. At the address position, the hands should be positioned about 2 to 4" closer to the target than the perpendicular line of the ball. This permits a more nearly perpendicular positioning of the clubface and decreases the chances of excessive lofting of the ball at contact.

Executing the Stroke

These points should be kept in mind when executing the chip shot (Figs. 8.5 and 8.6):

The stroke is basically a pendular movement with a minimum of wrist snap.

Figure 8.6 Chip shot: Initiating movement backward and follow-through to finish position.

There is a minimum of body turn in the takeback and only a slight body turn after the ball has taken flight.

The hands are kept ahead of the clubhead (the same relationship as at address) throughout the takeback and well through the point of impact.

The feel of the contact of the clubface of the ball gives an impression of a low-moving clubhead descending on the ball and continuing with a level movement along and through the flight line toward the target.

Well after impact and throughout the length of the follow-through, the player will make a conscious effort to keep the clubface in the perpendicular position as long as possible as well as at right angles to the flight line as far as the dropping point.

It is imperative to keep the head positioned and "anchored" over the perpendicular line of the ball throughout the takeback and well after impact of clubhead and ball. Chip shots can be spoiled by prematurely turning and lifting the head. This not only causes a jerky movement of the clubhead, resulting in a stab at the ball, but takes the player's concentration off the contact. This causes him to lose the feel of the clubhead movement at the moment critical to projecting the ball to the exact dropping spot.

THE PITCH SHOT

The purpose of the pitch shot is to project the ball high and have it land as close as possible to the flagstick or hole with the least possible roll of the ball after landing. Of the many factors that must be considered before deciding to play a pitch shot, these are some of the principal ones:

How far must the ball travel on the air?

How high a trajectory must be given the flight of the ball? Are there obstacles to travel over?

Is there any appreciable wind? Is it a head wind, a tail wind, or a cross wind?

What is the condition of the area where the ball is to land? Will the green hold the ball? Is the grass growing with the direction of the oncoming ball or against it? Is the green soft and damp, or hard and dry? Is there any contour to the green that will affect the roll of the ball after it lands?

Is the lie of the ball such as to permit uninterrupted contact of a lofted clubface with the ball? Variable conditions such as rough grass of hard ground upon which the ball lies should be carefully analyzed.

Only the most favorable conditions warrant a decision to play the high pitch shot. Adverse conditions should lead to choice of a more conservative play such as the chip shot (Figs. 8.7 and 8.8).

The Grip

The grip is the same as the overlap grip used in the full swing. In the modified pitch shot, sometimes referred to as the pitch-and-run shot, players often grip the club farther down on the handle much as in the chip shot.

Figure 8.7 Pitch shot: Addressing the ball through top of backswing.

The Stance

As in the chip shot, the open stance is recommended, except that a narrow stance is workable in the pitch-and-run shot. In the pitch-and-run shot, the ball may be positioned in a line that is ahead of the foot on the far side or one that is about equidistant between the feet. In the full pitch shot, a high trajectory is preferred, and it would be much easier to get this by positioning the stance so that the ball is in a line ahead of and a bit to the inside of the foot nearer the target. This latter position allows the clubface to contact the ball and take it on the uptake of the clubhead movement.

Executing the Swing

The execution of the full pitch shot is very similar to that of the full swing. The primary difference is in the length of the takeback, it being shortened and adjusted to correlate with the specific distance requirement of the shot. The modified pitch shot, the pitch-and-run variety, calls for a reduced takeback and follow-through that is a little longer than in the execution of the chip shot. The following points should be kept in mind when executing the pitch shot:

The basic points observed in the full swing should be followed in the full pitch shot.

Figure 8.8   Pitch shot: Impact through finish position.

The execution for all pitch shots is a smooth, unhurried swing of the clubhead. Although a high trajectory is desired, no forcing of the clubhead at impact should be attempted. The loft of the clubhead naturally imparts the necessary flight trajectory. Whipping the clubhead through at impact can cause seriously deviant contacts between clubface and ball.

In the hand action, the lower hand should come through fast but smoothly, so that at the moment of the impact of the clubface upon the ball, the upper and the lower hand are in a straight line from the grip, pointing downward to the center of the ball. There should be no attempt to force the hands to lift or scoop the clubhead.

The amount of divot taken depends upon the lie of the ball and the condition of the turf. The less the amount of divot taken, the less the clubhead is resisted in its movement through the ball. Too much divot taken reduces the velocity of the clubhead, thereby causing some loss of effective movement of the clubhead upward and through the ball.

Remember—it is the combination of all the natural conditions—the clubface, the lie, the condition of the grass, the wind, and the physical characteristics of the green—that determines the effectiveness of the pitch shot. Though the player executes the movement of the clubhead to strike the ball, he should learn to rely upon the clubhead to do the job. The clubface has two features that do the work: (1) the loft and (2) the grooves that grip the ball and increase the backspin.

IN THE SAND BUNKER: CHIP AND EXPLOSION SHOTS

The ways of playing from the sand bunker vary greatly, because playing conditions vary—the type of sand in the bunker, the lie of the ball, the distance the ball must travel, the trajectory necessary to clear the bunker, the condition of the putting green and so on. There is, however, only one objective—to get the ball out in one stroke. Basically, it is sufficient to depend upon two fundamental methods: (1) the chip shot and (2) the explosion shot. Occasionally, it may be judicious to play a full swing shot with a wood or a long iron, but only when the most ideal conditions prevail (see paragraph on fairway bunkers, Chapter 9).

Chipping from the sand bunker is workable when the lie is such that the ball is sitting high and clean on top of the sand and when the bunker is level enough so that playing a high trajectory shot out of the bunker is unnecessary. It might even be advisable to use the putter when the conditions warrant such a conservative play. The technique of chipping from the sand bunker is essentially the same as that for short chip shots from the fairway, with one additional important point to keep in mind: take the ball cleanly and crisply from the surface of the sand without lowering the clubhead into it. Follow through after the impact much as in chipping from the fairway. Because of the consistency of results with the chip shot, do not be ashamed to play this shot whenever the sand bunker conditions allow for it.

When the ball is partly or entirely buried in the sand, there is little choice but to explode into the sand with the clubhead and blast the ball out of the bunker. The special sand wedge, the pitching wedge, or the 9 iron (if a wedge is not available) are the best clubs to use. Figures 8.9 to 8.12 show explosion shots

Figure 8.9 Explosion shot: Addressing the ball.

from a bunker. These are the fundamental points to keep in mind:

Because of the non-grounding rule, be careful not to ground your club when addressing the ball.

Play the ball from a point between the center of your stance and the foot nearer the target — take an open stance.

Grip the club so that the face of the club is open enough to allow the edge at the bottom of the clubface, not the sole, to cut through the sand first.

Aim at a point behind the ball and into the sand. The force of the swing depends upon the lie and the distance to the green. The sand will raise the ball out of its buried lie, and the momentum of the clubhead swinging through and continuing upward will carry the ball the desired distance.

Execute the swing in a rather upright plane. This will allow a more abrupt follow-through in the natural course of the swing of the clubhead through the sand.

Follow through definitely. Do not let the clubhead sink into too much snad, and do not let it slow down while exploding through the sand. Doing this is what ruins most unsuccessful sand explosion shots.

Do not try to whip extra power into the explosion shot, for this invariably causes the clubhead to enter the sand at a wrong point — either too far back, or on top of the ball.

Figure 8.10 Explosion shot: Top of backswing through impact.

Figure 8.11 Explosion shot: Initiating the backswing and impact.

Figure 8.12 Sand explosion shot at impact.

Improving
Your
Game

Good scoring golf involves—in addition to swinging the clubs correctly—analysis, judgment, planning, and decision. A sound mechanical game depends upon sound strategy and management. Besides the fundamental factors of persistent practice, determination, concentration, relaxation, and coolheadedness, careful study of the following points and their application during play will go a long way toward improving scoring ability.

BASIC COURSE PLAY

Studying the Rules

Many situations arise in the course of a round of play that demand knowledgeable application of the rules. The best way to learn them and to keep abreast of changes in them is to carry a copy of the current edition of "The Rules of Golf" as published by the USGA. They are obtainable at golf course pro-shops and also directly from the United States Golf Association, 40 E. 38th St., New York, N.Y., 10016. Whenever opportunity arises, check directly with the rules book. If points of interpretation come up, check with the golf professionals in your area or with the local golf committee or association.

Strategy from the Teeing Ground

Do not always automatically tee up your ball at the midpoint between the tee markers. To tee up midway between the markers is all right if the hole is wide open, with no surrounding trouble. Most holes are laid out with some sort of challenge to the tee shot. It would be wiser to tee up on one side of the teeing ground, thus gaining the full advantage of aiming away from trouble. If there is trouble only on one side, tee up on the side of trouble and aim away from it. If there is trouble on both sides, make some allowance toward the side opposite the lesser of the two trouble problems. In this situation, select your club carefully and do not try for maximum distance. Be aware of the prevailing winds, but do not allow for them too much. The direction of a well hit ball is not altered more than a few yards by cross winds unless they are exceptionally strong.

Always take advantage of the teeing ground rule to tee up your ball. When using an iron, be sure that the tee is adequately but loosely embedded in the turf or ground. A tee that is too tightly embedded in hard-packed ground will tend to resist the movement of the clubhead upon impact, thus slowing it down or causing undesirable gyration of the ball.

Do not consciously force your execution in order to gain extra distance off the tee. After all, it is only the first of the strokes necessary to get down in par figure. Select a spot for your target off the tee and play to it. Accept the fact that you will have to play another stroke after the tee shot; so play it with the primary purpose of setting yourself up for the best possible position for your next shot.

Playing Out of the Rough

There is one axiom for this situation—accept your unlucky predicament and get out with the least number of strokes. If the situation is nearly impossible, declare the ball unplayable and accept the unplayable lie penalty, thus avoiding both the possibility of not getting out and also the risk of more strokes. Do not try for a miracle shot. If you decide upon playing from the lie, select your club with a single purpose—to get out to the nearest safe spot. Do not try for more distance than you can manage. Before you decide to play a bad lie from the rough, ask yourself these questions:

Can you negotiate an adequate backswing?

Is the ball clearly accessible? Can your clubhead get to it without interference and can your clubface make a definite contact with it?

Is there enough room for an adequate follow-through?

Are there obstacles the ball must clear when it travels on its way out of the rough?

Be honest in your answers to these questions. Remember—get out in one stroke! The worst that should happen is the cost of a stroke-and-distance penalty. You should not need to pay more.

Playing Out of Fairway Bunkers

Most fairway bunkers cause considerable trouble to the high-scoring player, because they notoriously appear flatter than they are. To clear the elevated border of the fairway bunker, the selection of a club with ample loft becomes critical. Another problem is the temptation to make up for lost distance. The high-scoring player invariably attempts to use a club for distance rather than one with ample loft. The prime strategy is to get out in one stroke. This may require the most conservative approach—playing a short chip shot or, if necessary, even a putt out of the flat side of the bunker. If the ball lies partly covered by the sand, then an explosion shot just to get the ball out of the bunker takes priority. The use of a wood or of a long iron may be attempted only under the most favorable conditions. Again, as in playing from the rough, play it smart and get out in one stroke, with only one thought in mind—to set up your next shot by playing this one safely.

Playing the Uphill Lie

Here two essential problems face the player: (1) position-ing stance in relation to the ball and (2) club selection. An uphill lie will generally require modification of the swing path of the clubhead so that the movement of the clubhead through impact and the follow-through will conform to the rising contour of the ground. Therefore, the ball should be played in a line off the foot nearer the target, that is, off the high side of the stance. Decide upon the distance and select a club that gives a straighter face, or less loft, than the one you would normally select to play the same distance. Do not be afraid to go as much as two clubs higher if the hill is exceptionally steep. The resultant trajectory of the ball will be higher, and therefore shorter. To offset this, select a lower-numbered club and concentrate upon executing the backswing and the follow-through in conformity with the contour of the ground.

Playing the Downhill Lie

This situation also presents the two essential problems of positioning stance in relation to the ball and of club selection. The ball should be played in a line off the foot farther away from the target, that is, off the high side of the stance. Decide upon the distance and select a club that gives more loft than the one you would normally select for the same purpose. The resultant trajectory of the ball will be a lower one, with the possibility, therefore, that the ball will roll more after landing. To offset this, select a higher-numbered club. In the follow-through immediately after impact, stay low on the swing path of the clubhead a little longer. This is necessary in order to avoid topping the ball.

Playing in Heavy Winds

Heavy winds will bother golfers who try to fight them. Instead, cope with them by learning a few basic guidelines. There are three wind problems: (1) the tail wind, (2) the head wind, and (3) the cross wind. In a tail wind, play to get the ball into the air, and it will give you more distance, if that is what you want. Play the ball from the forward part of the stance and use a club with loft one step more than normal. Do not expect the ball to bite or grab when approaching a green with a tail wind. Instead, allow for more than the normal amount of roll.

In a head wind, play to keep the ball in a lower trajectory by addressing it in line to the rear of center of the stance and by selecting a club with less loft. Do not expect the ball to roll the normal distance after landing. In approaching the green, if the play is with a pitch shot, play for a spot a few feet beyond the hole.

In a cross wind, make a slight alteration in lining up your aim, locating your target a little to the side of the direction from which the cross wind is coming. The wind will reduce the speed of the ball somewhat; so select a club stronger than normal for the distance. Play for the straight shot instead of trying to fade or draw into or with the wind. You will have a better run of the ball with the straight shot; that is, you will not risk having the ball run too far off line.

Analyzing the Conditions Surrounding Each Hole

A golfer scores best on his home course for one main reason—he has achieved a thorough analysis of all the conditions on the course. He is thoroughly acquainted with every contour on every green, every section of grass on every fairway, the exact distance between any two points of play, the prevailing and altering characteristics of the wind, and the location of all the trouble spots. He literally has a plan for each shot on every hole, for he has played each hole many times. These are the kinds of question he has found answers for on every hole:

Where is the best spot to play to from the teeing ground? Should I attempt to drive for maximum distance, or should I deliberately control my shot for placement? Which club should I use for the greatest consistency in management?

Which side of the fairway should I favor for the best chance of staying out of trouble? Are there out of bounds areas bordering the hole? Are there rough areas? Are there hazards? If there is a dog-leg, where is the best place to go in order to have the best setup for the next shot?

How is the wind blowing; is it steady and from a constant direction, or is it continually shifting?

Where is the best place to go in order to have the best approach to the green, to take advantage of the prevailing wind at the green, to avoid the risk of bunkers, to take into account water hazards and the like surrounding the green, to have the easiest recovery shot if I should miss the green on the approach shot?

Should the shot be made directly to the flagstick; are there dangerous risks in this? Or should the shot be played deliberately short, depending on a chip and a putt?

Is the green level with the fairway, or is it considerably elevated? (Note: with an elevated green, use a club one stronger than normal.)

Is the surface of the green level? Is there a contour? Which way does the green slope? What is the condition of the grass on the green; is the grain with the roll of my ball, against it, or cross-cut to it? Will the ball roll fast, moderately, or slowly over the surface of the green?

The strategic player, then, is the thoughtfully analytic player. He studies the conditions actually facing him on every stroke before he selects the club to play the shot. Every shot becomes a test of his judgment. With trial and error, lots of practice, sufficient experience on the golf course, and a sense of methodical and analytic review, he can learn to master his game and, with a little luck, perhaps the golf course too.

SUGGESTIONS FOR IMPROVEMENT

What to Do About the Slice

The generalized flight paths of the slice and of shots related to deviations to the right for the right-handed player are shown in Fig. 9.1. Going from left to right, flight path No. 1 is

the slice, No. 2 is the fade, No. 3 is the *push-fade*, and No. 4 is
the push-out. The slice may be attributed to one of two factors
or to a combination of the two: (1) the movement of the
clubhead through impact is in a path moving from the outside
of the flight line through the ball to the inside of the flight line
(this is commonly referred to as *cutting across* the flight line),
and (2) the angle of the clubface (the line from the heel to the
toe of the clubhead) is open to the target at impact. Figure 9.2
shows an overhead view of these two relationships. The line <u>P</u>
shows the path of the clubhead moving in an outside-in
direction across the flight line (see arrow). The symbol θ refers
to the angle of the clubface at impact. The series of small
arrows indicates the resultant rotation of the ball in a
left-to-right direction.

The outside-in path of the clubhead usually accompanies
an open stance, with the clubhead lifted outward and away
from the flight line in the backswing and coming down from the
top of the backswing from the outside of the flight line. At
impact, the hands are moving the handle (grip) of the club well
ahead of the clubhead. The lower hand is considerably behind
the lead hand, and both wrists are strongly abducted or cocked
toward the thumbs. The fade is produced by a relatively straight
path in the movement of the clubhead through the flight line at

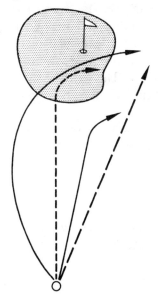

Figure 9.1   The slice: Flight path deviations.

impact, but the hands allow the clubface to strike the ball open to the target. The push-out variety is produced by a relatively slight inside-out path of the clubhead with the clubface angle squared to it.

To correct the slice: rely upon the parallel stance; in executing the swing of the clubhead, keep it as much as possible in the plane of the flight line through the impact; and in the hand action, have the lower hand directly under the lead hand at impact.

What to Do About the Hook

The hook may be thought of as the opposite of the slice. The generalized flight paths of the hook and of shots related to the hook (the draw, the pull, and the "pull-draw") for the right-handed player are shown in Fig. 9.3. Reading from right to left, flight path No. 1 is the hook; No. 2 is the draw; No. 3 is the pull-draw, and No. 4 is the pull. The hook may be attributed to one of two factors or to a combination of the two: (1) the movement of the clubhead through impact is in a path moving from the inside of the flight line through the ball and arcing around to the inside of the flight line, and (2) the angle of the clubface is closed to the target at impact. Figure 9.4 shows these two relationships from an overhead view. The line P designates the path of the clubhead moving in inside-around-and-in arc in relation to the perpendicular plane of the flight line that is indicated by the arrow. The symbol θ refers to the angle of the clubface at impact. The series of small arrows indicates the resultant rotation of the ball in a right-to-left direction.

The inside arcing of the clubhead path through to the inside of the flight line usually accompanies a closed stance,

Figure 9.2   Clubhead movement producing the slice.

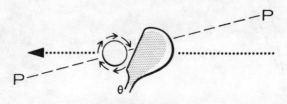

with the clubhead striking the ball well ahead of the hands at impact. The lower hand rolls over with the upper hand in a relatively collapsed state. A pronounced combination of these actions will produce a hook. The draw is produced by a relatively straight path in the movement of the clubhead through the flight line at impact, but the hands allow the clubhead to strike the ball slightly closed to the target. The pull variety is produced by a relatively straight line in the movement of the clubhead through a path that is outside-in, with the angle of the clubface closed to the flight line to the taget.

To correct the hook: rely upon the parallel stance; execute the swing of the clubhead through the impact, keeping it as much as possible in the plane of the flight line; and in the hand action, have the lower hand directly under the lead hand at impact.

The Intentional Low Ball

When playing into a head wind or under tree branches or against some similar obstacle, being able to play a low ball is welcome. The ball is struck at a point above its center, with the path of the clubhead moving as much as possible in a line

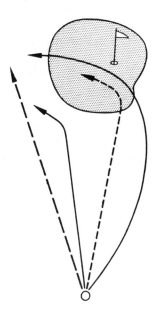

Figure 9.3 Hook flight path deviations.

parallel with the ground (Fig. 9.5). As the clubhead hits the ball, the wrists are held in vertical alignment to each other and in line with the vertical plane arising from the point of contact with the ball. The hands maintain this relationship through the impact and as long as possible during the follow-through. The follow-through is not arced upward; rather, an attempt is made to keep the hands from going above the horizontal level of the shoulders. Any of the following actions, accompanied by the execution just described, will aid in playing a low ball: playing the ball more in line with the back side of the stance (Fig. 9.6); positioning the hands at address so as to *hood* the clubface slightly; shifting the body weight over the foot on the near side immediately attending the impact; and keeping the body weight over that foot during the follow-through.

The Intentional High Ball

When in a tail wind or playing over trees or abrupt hills, the ability to finesse the execution so as to produce a high flying ball comes in handy. The ball is struck at a point below its center, with the path of the clubhead moving as much as possible in an arc that sweeps upward through the ball (Fig. 9.6). As the clubhead strikes the ball, the lower hand plays directly under the upper hand, with the palm of the lower hand facing upward. The wrist of the upper hand is bent fully toward the target, and the back of the hand faces upward. The clubhead is allowed to arc upward as high as possible in a smooth and uninterrupted flow of movement in the follow-through. Any of the following actions, accompanied by the execution just described, will aid in producing a high-flying ball: playing the ball more in line with the inside of the foot near the target (Fig. 9.6); positioning the hands at address so as to allow

Figure 9.4   Clubhead movement producing the hook.

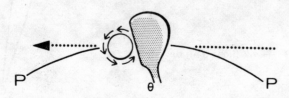

P   P

θ

the clubface to lie back a bit; deliberately shifting the body weight back to the foot on the far side immediately attending the impact; and allowing a slightly deeper than normal drop of the knee and shoulder on the far side.

HINTS ON HOW TO PRACTICE

When working at the practice tee, pick out appropriate targets and play a variety of shots with different clubs. Concentrate upon definite fundamental movements and insist upon achieving a definite sense of kinesthetic response to each stroke. Work on delivery of the clubhead and develop your sense of the feel of its movement throughout the swing. By all means, resist every temptation to slug it out for distance. Make every effort to attain control.

When practicing on the golf course, work on the conscious process of going through a definite pattern as follows:

Figure 9.5   Playing the intentional low ball.

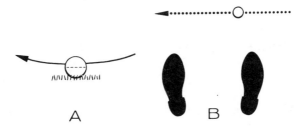

Figure 9.6   Playing the intentional high ball.

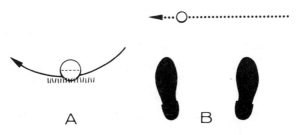

1. Analyzing the conditions.

Stance and lie. Note carefully the type of grass and the specific condition of the turf or sand—that is, analyze the ground for your stance and the lie of the your ball.

Wind. Make an accounting of the wind as to direction and velocity. Do this at the lie and also check the conditions out at the target.

Safety margin. Decide which side of the fairway or green offers the greatest margin of safety.

Playing distance. Note the distance accurately, taking into account slopes, the grain of the grass, and the firmness of the ground.

2. Preparing the address.

Club selection. Select the club and convert all the above analysis into a flight pattern for the shot.

Delivery point. From behind the ball, pick out a delivery point ahead of the ball as a guide through which to execute the delivery of the clubhead immediately after impact.

Feel of hands. Take a mental preview of the swing to acquire the actual feel of the shot. Emphasize the feel with your hands, since they will direct the shot.

3. Executing the address and the swing.

Swing tempo. Give attention to feeling the entire swing pattern and its tempo. Emphasize control and finesse for the exact distance contemplated. Take a practice swing to do this. Keep the head reasonably still.

Visual attention and focus. Emphasize visual attention to the ball and learn to extend this focus of attention through the ball to the delivery point.

Firm brace at impact. At impact, attend to the delivery of the clubhead through the delivery point and maintain a firm "bracing" quality with the entire near side.

Clubhead alignment. Check the alignment of the clubhead at the terminal point of the follow-through. The path and direction of the clubhead will indicate the probable flight pattern your ball will take.

4. Repeating for correction.

Repeat shots. Whenever possible, play a second shot immediately following the original shot, to correct mistakes in execution or errors in judgment. Immediate or spontaneous attempts to correct faults are extremely beneficial to improvement in technique and ability.

EXERCISES TO IMPROVE THE BASIC SWING

Two exercises are proposed here to help maintain, in addition to developmental value, a special degree of neuromuscular fitness specifically for the execution of the basic golf swing.

Lead-arm Swing

Figure 9.7 shows the performance of swinging a high-numbered club (7 iron) with only the lead arm executing the swing. Whenever possible, hit some balls this way and pay attention to the resultant flights. At first try, this maneuver seems hopelessly impossible to perform. Persist at it, and you will find that it soon becomes the best thing you can do to improve your swing.

Trail-arm Swing

Figure 9.8 shows the performance of swinging a high-numbered club (7 iron) with only the trail arm executing the swing. Throughout the exercise movement, hold the lead arm extended, with the hand placed in the air at front horizontal position and held in line above the ball. Again, it is extremely helpful actually to hit balls while performing this exercise. You will soon learn to develop the proper control in the use of the lower hand by attempting to execute the exercise with the production of good ball-flight responses.

An additional word about exercises. A round of golf in itself, though taxing nervous energy, does not offer enough exercise to the young or middle-aged person as to minimal and general physical fitness requirements. When one uses the pushcart or the motorized golf cart, the amount of exercise is further reduced. Additional effort in fitness exercises such as jogging is recommended.

Figure 9.7   Lead-arm swing exercise: Starting backswing through impact.

Figure 9.8 Trail-arm swing exercise: Starting position through impact.

Suggested
Readings

"All About Putting." *Golf Magazine,* 5, no. 5 (1963), pp.18-40. Articles by prominent professionals covering all aspects of putting.

American Association for Health, Physical Education, Recreation, *Group Golf Instruction for Beginners.* Washington, D.D., 1965. A planning guide by a committee of successful leaders to provide practical suggestions for initiating group instruction in golf, physical education, and recreation.

Altman, Dick and editors, *Golf Digest. The Square-To-Square Golf Swing.* Norwalk, Conn. Golf Digest, 1970. A presentation involving detailed analysis of such fundamentals as correct gripping and setting up to the ball, as well as actual swing instruction explained as a total concept.

Baymiller, John. "The Theory of Dimples for Distance." *Golf Digest,* (1963), pp.68-71. A description of how the depressions on a golf ball's surface affect its flight.

Boros, Julius. "Play the Course, Don't Attack It." *Golf Digest* 14, no. 1 (1964), pp.24-29. A discussion of strategy in playing from the teeing ground and in playing approach shots to the green.

Casper, Bill. *Chipping and Putting.* New York: Ronald Press Co., 1961. A thorough presentation of techniques and strategy in the vital short game of chipping and putting.

Cochran, Alastair and Stobbs, John. *The Search for the Perfect Swing.* London: Morrison and Gibb, 1968. Based on a scientific study commissioned by the Golf Society of Great Britain. Contains hundreds of stroboscopic photographs.

The Easy Way to Learn Golf Rules. National Golf Foundation, 804 Merchandise Mart, Chicago, Ill. An illustrated and interpretative discussion of the most frequent occurrences in playing situations requiring correct knowledge of golf rules.

Golf Digest Trilogy. So. Norwalk, Conn. Golf Digest, 1963. Three complete books: Sam Snead, *The Driver Book;* Doug Ford, *The Wedge Book;* Bob Rosburg, *The Putter Book.* Each carries a complete analysis of the clubs and their uses.

Griffin, C. W. "Backspin, How it Works, How to Make it Work for You." *Golf Magazine* 14, no. 5 (1972), pp.60-64, 116-19. An incisive explanation of a golf ball impact-and-flight phenomenon called backspin which we all seek and can have.

Jones, Robert T., Jr. "Improving Your Golf Through Management," *The Golf Journal USGA* 25, no. 1 (1972), pp.18-22. A forthright explanation of what makes a good golf game based upon the concept that hitting the ball properly and playing the game properly are quite distinct from one another.

Mr. X. *Golf Lessons with Mr. X,* Norwalk, Conn.: Golf Digest, 1968. Written by an unusually practical businessman who took up golf at age 43 and at 50 was playing scratch golf.

Nicklaus, Jack. *Take a Tip from Me.* New York: Simon and Schuster, 1968. Technical explanations of how to better your swing, strategical explanations of how to prepare yourself mentally for your round of golf, and practical explanations of how to play situation shots.

The Official Rules of Golf. United States Golf Association, 40 E. 38th., New York, N.Y., 1972. Covers all aspects of the official rules of the game.

Student/Teacher
Instructional Objectives

Comments on the Use of the Student/Teacher Evaluation Forms

The forms which follow were designed to be used in a variety of instructional settings. Preplanning and organization are necessary for these devices to be used as effectively as possible. The purpose of evaluation is for gauging how well the course objectives are accomplished. That is, evaluation will indicate the progress and the extent to which learning has occurred.

Although the learner *must do his own learning*, the teacher's role is to guide and to direct learning experiences and to provide for appropriate measurement procedures. The charts which follow have been constructed to place primary responsibility on the individual student for estimating progress and indicating areas which need work. It may not be either necessary or desirable to use all the materials provided here in a given teaching learning situation. The instructor and the student should work together to select the materials most appropriate for the course.

It must be remembered that sufficient time for practice and study must be provided if the individual is to perfect his skills as well to accrue knowledge and to develop understanding. The time available may not be adequate for *all* students to demonstrate acceptable levels of skill performance. The instructor may wish to supplement the evaluation devices with a written test covering analysis of performance, procedures, and rules. (Sample tests will be available in a separate instructor's manual covering the entire Goodyear Physical Activities series.) The written test provides an opportunity for the student to demonstrate his knowledge and understanding of the skill even though his actual skill might be less than desired. Final evaluation for grading purposes should take into account a number of variables which may have an influence on individual performance.

STUDENT	THE GRIP	TEACHER
_____	Left Hand	_____
_____	Right Hand	_____
_____	Overlap	_____
_____	Interlocking	_____
_____	Baseball	_____
_____	TOTAL EFFICIENCY	_____

THE STANCE

STUDENT		TEACHER
_____	Parallel	_____
_____	Open	_____
_____	Closed	_____
_____	TOTAL EFFICIENCY	_____

THE SWING

Backswing

STUDENT		TEACHER
_____	Posture At Address	_____
_____	Take Away	_____
_____	Left Arm	_____
_____	Right Arm	_____
_____	Hands	_____
_____	Wrists	_____
_____	Left Shoulder	_____
_____	Right Shoulder	_____
_____	Left Knee	_____
_____	Right Knee	_____
_____	Weight Shift	_____
_____	Head Position	_____
_____	TOTAL EFFICIENCY	_____

Class _____

Student _____

Teacher _____

Date _____

STUDENT **Position At The Top** TEACHER

_____ Posture _____

_____ Left Arm _____

_____ Right Arm _____

_____ Hands _____

_____ Wrists _____

_____ Left Shoulder _____

_____ Right Shoulder _____

_____ Left Knee _____

_____ Right Knee _____

_____ Weight Distribution _____

_____ Head Position _____

_____ TOTAL EFFICIENCY _____

Downswing

_____ Posture _____

_____ Left Arm _____

_____ Right Arm _____

_____ Hands _____

_____ Wrists _____

_____ Left Shoulder _____

_____ Right Shoulder _____

_____ Left Foot _____

_____ Right Foot _____

_____ Weight Shift _____

_____ Head Position _____

_____ TOTAL EFFICIENCY _____

Class _____

Student _____

Teacher _____

Date _____

STUDENT	Impact	TEACHER
_____	Left Arm	_____
_____	Right Arm	_____
_____	Hands	_____
_____	Wrists	_____
_____	Left Shoulder	_____
_____	Right Shoulder	_____
_____	Left Knee	_____
_____	Right Knee	_____
_____	Alignment	_____
_____	Head Position	_____
_____	Hips	_____
_____	TOTAL EFFICIENCY	_____

STUDENT	Follow-through	TEACHER
_____	Posture	_____
_____	Left Arm	_____
_____	Right Arm	_____
_____	Hands	_____
_____	Wrists	_____
_____	Left Shoulder	_____
_____	Right Shoulder	_____
_____	Left Foot	_____
_____	Right Foot	_____
_____	Weight Shift	_____
_____	Head Position	_____
_____	Hips	_____
_____	TOTAL EFFICIENCY	_____

Class _____

Student _____

Teacher _____

Date _____

STUDENT   ## PUTTING   TEACHER

Grip

STUDENT		TEACHER
_____	Reverse Overlap	_____
_____	Overlap	_____
_____	Interlocking	_____
_____	Baseball or other	_____
_____	Fingers	_____
_____	Palms	_____
_____	TOTAL EFFICIENCY	_____

Stance

_____	Head Position	_____
_____	Alignment	_____
_____	Weight Distribution	_____
_____	Clubface Alignment	_____
_____	TOTAL EFFICIENCY	_____

Stroke

_____	Wrists	_____
_____	Arms	_____
_____	Arms and Wrists	_____
_____	Take Away	_____
_____	Stroke	_____
_____	Impact	_____
_____	Follow-through	_____
_____	TOTAL EFFICIENCY	_____

Class _____

Student _____

Teacher _____

Date _____

STUDENT	CHIP SHOT	TEACHER

STUDENT

CHIP SHOT

TEACHER

_____ Club Choice _____

_____ Grip _____

_____ Stance _____

_____ Execution _____

_____ TOTAL EFFICIENCY _____

PITCH SHOT

_____ Club Choice _____

_____ Grip _____

_____ Stance _____

_____ Execution _____

_____ TOTAL EFFICIENCY _____

SAND SHOT

_____ Chip _____

_____ Explosion _____

_____ Grip _____

_____ Stance _____

_____ Execution _____

_____ TOTAL EFFICIENCY _____

PROBLEM SHOTS

Uphill Lie

_____ Stance _____

_____ Club Selection _____

_____ TOTAL EFFICIENCY _____

Class _____

Student _____

Teacher _____

Date _____

STUDENT		TEACHER

Downhill Lie

_____ Stance _____

_____ Club Selection _____

_____ TOTAL EFFICIENCY_____

Heavy Winds

_____ Tail Wind _____

_____ Head Wind _____

_____ Cross Wind _____

_____ Stance _____

_____ Club Selections _____

_____ TOTAL EFFICIENCY_____

The Fade

_____ Grip _____

_____ Stance _____

_____ Swing _____

_____ TOTAL EFFICIENCY_____

The Draw

_____ Grip _____

_____ Stance _____

_____ Swing _____

_____ TOTAL EFFICIENCY_____

Intentional Low Ball

_____ Grip _____

_____ Stance _____

_____ Club Selection _____

_____ Swing _____

_____ TOTAL EFFICIENCY_____

Class _____

Student _____

Teacher _____

Date _____

STUDENT   **Intentional High Ball**   TEACHER

_____ Grip _____

_____ Stance _____

_____ Club Selection _____

_____ Swing _____

_____ TOTAL EFFICIENCY _____

GENERAL PLAYING STRATEGY

_____ Attacking _____

_____ Safe _____

_____ Gambler _____

_____ Thinker _____

_____ Fire and Fall Back _____

_____ Course Player _____

_____ Opponent Player _____

_____ TOTAL EFFICIENCY _____

Class _____

Student _____

Teacher _____

Date _____